A WURLD OF
Choice,

A WORLD OF
Freedom

by Gary M. Douglas

A World Of Choice A World Of Freedom

ISBN: 978-1-63493-155-7

For questions, please contact:
Access Consciousness Publishing
406 Present Street
Stafford, TX 77477 USA
accessconsciousnesspublishing.com

Your life doesn't have to be about limitation.

It doesn't have to be about creating
the same old thing.

Your choice can change anything.

Gary M. Douglas

FOREWORD

THE ACCESS CONSCIOUSNESS CLEARING STATEMENT®

This book about choice, possibility, and freedom is based on a series of four telecalls I did with an awesome group of participants who asked great questions and brought a wonderful energy to our conversations.

During the course of our calls, we did lots of clearings, which we've included in this book. I encourage you to do them, as well. If you are new to the Access Consciousness Clearing Statement, you can read about what the words mean and how it works at the end of this book.[1] The clearing statement goes like this:

> *Right and Wrong, Good and Bad, POD and POC, All 9, Shorts, Boys, and Beyonds.*®

When you first read the clearing statement, it may twist your head around a little bit. That's our intention. It's designed to get your mind out of the picture so you can get to the energy of a situation. With the clearing statement, we're not addressing what we *think* about a situation; we're addressing the *energy* of the limitations and barriers that keep us from moving forward and expanding into all the spaces we would like to go.

I invite you to ask yourself the questions given in the book and to do the clearings, preferably several times over, because as you do, you open the door to creating from a different place.

---

1 If you'd like more information about the clearing statement, you can visit: https://www.accessconsciousness.com/theclearingstatement

The clearings from each call are given at the end of each chapter so you can review and repeat them. I also recommend that you return to each chapter a day or a week or a month after you've completed it, to re-read the text and go through the clearings and questions again.

As you do this, you will begin to see things from a different point of view. Possibilities will appear that you wouldn't have recognized before. A new reality will start to show up in your life in ways you would never have expected.

You've had billions of years of creating your life as misery, so you might need to do the questions and clearings several times. Try it and see if it works for you.

TABLE OF CONTENTS

THE FIRST CALL

Choice Creates

You need to choose in order to become aware.

Begin to see what is actually possible for you.

Your choice is all it takes to create it.

ONLY BY OUR CHOICE DO WE CREATE SOMETHING

Gary: Hello, everyone. Welcome to our telecall series, A World of Choice, A World of Freedom.

The greatest freedom you have available to you in life is the ability to choose.

Choice is innate to us, and only by our choice do we create something. Choice creates. Through choice we learn how to expand the elements of life we wish to have.

Here's an example: Henry, our horse trainer in Costa Rica, used to expect me to give him things, and for the longest time he didn't have any gratitude for me. Then somewhere along the line, he started developing gratitude for me, and the last time we were in Costa Rica, he gave me a beautiful new saddle. It's a gorgeous saddle, one of the best I've seen in Costa Rica. And when I gave him a compliment about his capacity with horses and his ability to do things other people can't do, he received that compliment for the first time ever. People noticed those things and commented on them.

I asked, "Why is he receiving the compliment now?" It was because he chose gratitude sufficiently to create it as a reality. You can do this, too. Every time you choose something, you expand your capacity for choice. If you're willing to be grateful for somebody, by constantly being in a state of gratitude, you expand your capacity for gratitude.

Your choice creates your reality. You have to choose the reality you want. Every time you have an opportunity for something, you have to look at it and ask:

- What do I want to choose?

- What do I want to create as my reality?

These two questions will give you the greatest possibility in life.

EVERY CHOICE YOU MAKE CREATES A DIFFERENT POSSIBILITY

Call Participant: Can you describe what being willing to choose is? I wonder whether I'm doing it correctly.

Gary: I can tell you that you are not doing it correctly—because you're wondering whether you're doing it correctly rather than realizing that every choice you make creates a different possibility. Choice doesn't equal a right or wrong.

Please stop trying to choose *correctly!* Stop looking for *correct* choice! When you look for correct choice, everything you're doing is about choosing that which this reality defines as right or wrong. There's more than a little bit of unconsciousness connected to that.

> *How many choices are you using to create the right and wrong of this reality as the only choice, the no-choice universe you are choosing? Everything that is times a godzillion, will you destroy and uncreate it all? Right and Wrong, Good and Bad, POD and POC, All 9, Shorts, Boys, and Beyonds.*

When you realize that every choice you make creates the future you're going to experience, you begin to recognize: "Oh! This is what choice creates." For example, if you choose to marry somebody, have you made a choice? Yes. What choice did you make? You didn't just choose marriage. You chose a particular life.

Many years ago, I chose to marry a woman who had the point of view that the way to get money was to spend everything you had. It was: "In order to have money, you have to get rid of money. That way you create a vacuum so more money can come in." What?! She didn't get that her choice meant we never had money.

What if your choice is the source of creation? It is! When you get that, you will look at what's being created by your choices, and then, if you wish, you can choose something different. What would happen if you were willing to do that? Choose something, look at what is being created by that choice, and ask: "What can be chosen different?"

What if you were willing to look at every choice you made for the possibility of what it would create? What if you were willing to ask, for every choice you make: "What possibilities will I create by this choice?" Choice is asking:

- What am I going to create?
- What's my future going to be, based on my choice?

It's a whole different universe when you start to get: "Something else is possible here I haven't considered."

YOUR CHOICE CREATES YOUR REALITY

Call Participant: How can we use choice in a pragmatic way?

Gary: Recognize that choice creates. For everything you have created that you don't like, ask:

- What choices did I make that created this as reality?

- What choices did I make that created the reality about me that I do not desire or like?
- What choices did I make that created the reality about me I am not happy with?

If your reality is not what you want it to be, there's something you are choosing or have chosen that you're not willing to let go of. You've got to be willing to look at whatever choice you've made that is creating what's going on. Ask: "What choices did I make that are creating or created this?"

Look at this in terms of your money situation. Are you happy with your money situation? No?

What choices did you make that created the reality about you and your money you do not desire, like, or are happy with? Everything that is times a godzillion, will you destroy and uncreate it all? Right and Wrong, Good and Bad, POD and POC, All 9, Shorts, Boys, and Beyonds.

Let's do that again:

What choices did you make that created the reality about you and your money you do not desire, like, or are happy with? Everything that is times a godzillion, will you destroy and uncreate it all? Right and Wrong, Good and Bad, POD and POC, All 9, Shorts, Boys, and Beyonds.

And once more:

What choices did you make that created the reality about you and your money you do not desire, like, or are happy with? Everything that is times a godzillion, will you destroy and uncreate it all? Right and Wrong, Good and Bad, POD and POC, All 9, Shorts, Boys, and Beyonds.

BECOMING BRILLIANT WITH MONEY

Call Participant: What would it take for brilliance with money to be a choice for me?

Gary: It's clear, from that question alone, that you have already decided you can't be brilliant. You've decided you have no choice. Ask: "What would I have to be or do different to have the brilliance with money I truly be?" Do you notice the difference in energy between that question and the one you asked?

If you could have financial brilliance, what would that look like? You have no bloody clue because you have not exercised your willingness to be aware of what's happening financially that other people don't get. You're not willing to recognize, "Wait a minute! I'm way better than other people."

If you really want to be brilliant with money, you have to be willing to educate yourself about money. People think I'm pretty brilliant with money. I'm not the most brilliant, but I don't do without, which is really nice, and I manage to create amazing things. I went from no money when I started Access to making a whole bunch of money each year, and because of my willingness to have money, there are a lot of people who also make a lot of money by working with us.

If you're going to make a lot of money, you have to be willing to support others with money. That's one of the brilliances with money that most of us are not willing to have. You have to ask: "How can I use the money I have to support people who can facilitate a greater reality?" These are the people who I support and who I pay and who work with me.

Brilliance with money is knowing what you can do with money to create a different reality. Most people are not willing to have that; they're not willing to educate themselves about money. Are you aware, for example, that banking corporations are not there to help you? They're there to find ways to take your money. Most people are not willing to look at or make themselves aware of this kind of stuff.

What have you been unwilling to see, do, perceive, know, be, and receive about the choices you make that keep you from having everything you desire? Will you destroy and uncreate all that please? Right and Wrong, Good and Bad, POD and POC, All 9, Shorts, Boys, and Beyonds.

Nice, eh? Let's do it again:

What have you been unwilling to see, do, perceive, know, be, and receive about the choices you make that keep you from having everything you desire? Will you destroy and uncreate all that please? Right and Wrong, Good and Bad, POD and POC, All 9, Shorts, Boys, and Beyonds.

YOU HAVE TO CHOOSE TO CREATE GREATER AMOUNTS OF MONEY

Gary: Ask: "What would I have to be or do different that would allow me to have the brilliance of money I truly be?" Ask it often. I am always looking for what I can be or do different that will create more money in my life.

Look at your life and ask:

- Do I have all the money I desire?
- Have I created some money?
- Is it enough?
- Okay, if I have created the amount I have, is it possible I could create more?
- What choice would I have to make to create way more than this?

You have to *choose* to create greater amounts of money. You cannot just ask for it and wish for it. If wishes were horses then beggars would ride and drink rum. You've got to look from a different point of view. I was able to create Access because I've chosen my life in ways that other people never choose.

For example, I started investing in antiques years ago, because I knew they were a gift. Recently I met with Chris, who manages my antique business in Australia, and we talked about the difficulty with the antique business today: Everybody who is in it is old. Everybody who is brilliant at it is old. All the investors are old.

What is not being looked at today is that for centuries, older people have always been willing to look at what is intrinsically valuable. That's not occurring right now. Everyone is looking for the technology and their "dot com" business that's going to make them millionaires. They're not looking to have intrinsic wealth or to create wealth.

You've also got to be willing to work or to do whatever it takes to get what you want. In the early 1970s, I had a back operation. I couldn't work and I was getting disability payments. I had saved a total of $7,000, and I said, "I'm going to Europe." Everyone in my family thought I was nuts. Their point of view was: "Why would you ever leave the United States? It's got everything."

So I went to Europe. I thought, "I'm going be here for six months." Did I think $7,000 was going to last me six months? Sure. Why not? I decided it would. Well, that didn't happen, but I was willing to work or do whatever it took to get what I wanted. And by the choices I made, I always got what I wanted ... if I was willing to do whatever it took to get it. That choice created the path of my life.

WHAT IF YOU USED YOUR MONEY TO CREATE MORE POSSIBILITY?

Call Participant: I had an awesome conversation with a friend last night. I was speaking with him about my desire to use everything I know to create more money. He asked, "What would having more money create for you?"

Gary: What's the purpose of money for you?

Call Participant: I'm going to say, "To create more freedom." I've never said that before.

Gary: Freedom is possibility. What if you used your money to create more possibility? That's what I do. You've got to use your money. Money is something you use to create other possibilities. Ask: "If I do this, what possibilities will it create?"

Call Participant: I have never equated creating more possibility with freedom.

Gary: When you have the freedom of possibility and you look for what else is possible, you are seeking that which is the creation of a different reality.

Look at what's possible. It's about asking: "What's possible for me that's not possible for others?" You have made choices in every lifetime that have taken you to a place where you have possibilities that other people do not have. That is why you're able to create and generate what you have. That's why you're able to choose to create a different reality.

What is possible that you haven't even considered? What would it look like if you were willing to be aware of all that? What could you have that would be different? Be willing to look at everything from a different point of view. Ask:

- What do I really want to create here?
- What do I want to create for me?

When you are willing to go beyond what other people are capable of, you begin to be aware of possibilities other people can't choose.

Choice creates freedom. What freedom occurs from choice? The fact that you can choose again! What kind of freedom do you get from having money? The willingness to choose things other people cannot choose. Oh! So what else is possible that you haven't even considered? What would it be like if you were willing to open the door to nothing more than greater and greater possibility?

The ability to choose the possibilities that exist in the world is the gift you came into this life with.

What possibilities are you refusing that you really could be choosing that if you would choose them would create a different reality for you in every aspect of your life? Everything that is times a godzillion, will you destroy and uncreate it all? Right and Wrong, Good and Bad, POD and POC, All 9, Shorts, Boys, and Beyonds.

And again:

What possibilities are you refusing that you really could be choosing that if you would choose them would create a different reality for you in every aspect of your life? Everything that is times a godzillion, will you destroy and uncreate it all? Right and Wrong, Good and Bad, POD and POC, All 9, Shorts, Boys, and Beyonds.

"WAIT A MINUTE. WHAT DO I TRULY DESIRE?"

Call Participant: I recently realized that a lot of what I thought I desired isn't actually true. What can I be or do different to create everything I *truly* desire?

Gary: You make a choice and then you may get to a point where you say, "Wait a minute. I don't actually desire this." I got married the first time because I was involved in a cult that said, "Only if you're married and have children are you a 'real' person." I wanted to be a real person, so I got married and had children. Then, after the fact, I realized, "Wait a minute! I was a real person before I got married! There is nothing wrong with me! I am not nearly as screwed up as half the people in this organization who think they're not screwed up because they're in this organization! It's so screwed up!"

Call Participant: Is that one of the times you would say, "Choice creates awareness"? I've chosen things based on what I thought I desired then I got more awareness and I realized, "That's not what I desire." Now it's more about "What do I *truly* desire?"

TEN-SECOND INCREMENTS OF CHOICE

Gary: Yes, you say, "I made a choice. It was a bad choice. What would I like to choose now? What do I truly desire and what would I like to choose now—in this ten seconds?" Ten-second increments of choice is one of the keys to unlocking everything you desire in life.

Choosing in ten-second increments is about being present for every moment of your life. Most people, rather than being present, try to create a plan and a system for the future so it will show up the way they want it. Once they do that, they think they don't need to be aware any longer. Big mistake. When you choose in ten-second increments, you get to choose, and choose again, and in so doing, you create choice and the opportunity to receive infinite possibilities.

KIDS CAN CHOOSE AGAIN, TOO

Call Participant: Things are not going well with me and my daughter. Today she left the house and said, "I'm going to live with my father!" For the first time, I'm not trying to save her from her choice. What question can I ask here? She's still my daughter. I love her.

Gary: With my kids, I learned to say, "I love you totally, no matter how stupid you are. No matter how crazy you are, I still love you." When you get that you can love somebody no matter how stupid and crazy their choices are, it's because you have the awareness that they can always choose different. You are aware they can choose again and that they've never really chosen against themselves.

My kids have done things that I thought were damn stupid and strange, and I have made the mistake of asking them, "Why the hell would you choose that?" Never ask your kids that question! Instead I learned to ask: "So how's that working out for you?" and they'd tell me how they decided their choice was going to work out. I would get the awareness that it was not going to turn out that way, and I'd say, "Oh well," because I knew they would gain awareness by the choices they made.

Will your daughter gain awareness from the choice of going to live with her father? Yes. Will she find out that he's not nearly as good as he says he is? Yes. And of course, fathers are much less controlling than mothers, aren't they?

Her choice is going to give her a lot of awareness about what works and what doesn't work. The one thing I can guarantee is that her father will pretend to allow her to have a lot of freedom and not give it to her. Fathers are far less tolerant and in allowance of little trollops being trollops than mothers are. Within six months, she'll probably be asking, "Mum, can I move back in with you? Dad's an asshole!"

BY THE CHOICES YOU MAKE YOUR AWARENESS GROWS

Gary: Have you ever gone to bed with someone you should never have gone to bed with?

Call Participant: Who me? Never!

Gary: By that choice, did you become aware of something? Yes.

We often misidentify awareness as *learning*. We think we *learned* something, not that we became *aware* of something. If you misidentify and misapply awareness as learning, instead of being aware, you try to learn. *Learning* is always about buying data from other people. That's totally different from *being aware*.

You're aware of energies, and by the choices you make, your awareness grows. Every time you choose for awareness, your awareness grows. So don't make your choices based on what you have *learned*; make your choices based on what you are *aware* of. Ask:

- What awareness can I have here?
- What can I be that would create a different possibility?

Do that and all kinds of things will show up for you.

Every choice you have made in your life has created who you are. You have created you as the being you are, based on your choices. Does anybody else have the same choices or the same capacities you have? No. You're the only one of *you* that exists, because you're the only one who has chosen what you've chosen to get where you are. This is what makes you a unique being on planet Earth. Choice creates. It creates *you*. It creates what you are. It creates what you can do and what you can choose.

Ask: "What choice do I have that nobody else has?" When you ask that, you're not going to get an answer, but you are going to get an awareness. And with that awareness and the willingness to choose beyond what other people are capable of, you change the world for the realities you want to create.

YOU ARE THE CREATOR OF YOUR OWN REALITY

Gary: Early on in my life I created comfort and ease without having money. I managed to get the best places to live and to have beautiful things in my life. I had better furniture, china, and crystal than anybody I knew, and I had created a life that was easy. And then one day I asked, "If I can create comfort and ease with no money, what could I create if I was willing to have money?"

You are the creator of your own reality. You have created the reality you're currently living in because of your choices—not because of the wrongness of you, not because of the stupidity of you, not because you have lessons to learn. You've created your reality because you have choice.

Each individual comes in with the innate ability to choose— and nothing else. Every choice you make creates the way everything else shows up around you. You have to be willing to be that which chooses something nobody else can choose.

What can nobody else choose that you have never acknowledged you can choose that if you acknowledged you could choose it would change reality with every choice you make? Everything that is times a godzillion, will you destroy and uncreate it all? Right and Wrong, Good and Bad, POD and POC, All 9, Shorts, Boys, and Beyonds.

What can nobody else choose that you have never acknowledged you can choose that if you acknowledged you could choose it would change reality with every choice you made in every moment of every day? Everything that is times a godzillion, will you destroy and uncreate it all? Right and Wrong, Good and Bad, POD and POC, All 9, Shorts, Boys, and Beyonds.

CHOOSE THAT WHICH WORKS FOR YOU

Gary: Recently I thought, "It would be great to make good money doing 'normal' real estate." I looked at a house priced at $132,000 that was worth $165,000. For an investment of $10,000, I could buy it, rent it out, and have a cash flow of $400 a month, which would be close to $5,000 a year, and I would create $20,000 in equity.

Then I thought, "I would never live in a place like that. Do I want to promote people living in a place like that? No. Why wouldn't I want to live like that? Because I don't!" Is living like that right or wrong? Or is it just choice?

I was going to have to hold on to it for a while so it could go up in value. Are things going up in value in Houston? Yeah, big time. Would I have made money? You bet. My point of view was: "Yeah, but who cares? That's not my criterion for a great life."

I did not want to be the custodian of that property because I have the point of view that if you are living some place that is beautiful and wonderful, you have the ability to create. If you are living in a place that is not wonderful, you lose the ability to create.

That was one of the choices I made for myself. I wanted to live my life in a beautiful place, with beautiful things. That has run my life to a huge degree; I want beautiful things. I want a beautiful space. I wish to create a space that invites people to greater possibility, always. For me, nothing much other than that is worth having. I realized I had made a financial decision back in my early days that I wasn't even aware of. I thought I could do "normal" real estate the way a normal person does. But I can't! And it's not just that I can't; it's that I won't.

When I first started out in life, I rented a duplex that was on the edge of a farm. It was basically a pit, an ugly place in terrible condition. I started fixing it up so I could have something that would be more fun for me. I've done that with every house I've ever lived in. I would fix it up with my own money and my own volition, even when I was just renting, because I wanted it to be good for me. I discovered that landlords don't much care what you do to their house as long as you don't make it worse. I improved every place I lived and my landlords loved me. Why? I never charged them for the work I did.

I paid for what I did because I wanted it for me, and I wasn't going to ask them to do what I wanted. I was prepared to do whatever it took to get what I wanted. That's one of the criteria with which I have created financial wealth. I'm willing to do what works for me. I'm going to choose that which works for me because that gives me the freedom to choose. My choices are to stay or go, to contribute or not, and I became aware that my choice will always create what I desire if I am willing to choose it.

ALWAYS MAKE THE CHOICE TO SEEK SOMETHING GREATER

I once went to New York City and met a man who was living in a rent-controlled apartment. It was a beautiful pre-war building with high ceilings, beautiful moldings, wonderful windows— and the place was a total pit. I said, "You've been living here for ten years. Why haven't you painted?"

He said, "I know it's ugly and depressing, but I don't want the landlord to benefit from what I do."

I said, "You'll suffer in an ugly place so the landlord doesn't benefit? What difference does that make? You're the one living here. When do you get to benefit from where you live?"

I did not understand his point of view, because my choice would be to fix it up and make it as beautiful as it could be because I was living there. I'd say, "Hey, I have a rent-controlled apartment for $600 a month, three bedrooms, two baths, a dining room, living room, and kitchen. It's an awesome place in an awesome section of town where I have a really good time!"

He wasn't willing to paint his place because he didn't want to let somebody else make money. That was a choice he made: "I will never let anyone make money off me," and therefore, he could not expand his financial reality beyond a certain point. The choices we make and the decisions that follow them determine the kind of life we can have and be.

Have you realized that your choices are the source of creation? If you haven't realized this, you won't try to make choices that will lead beyond what anybody else could imagine. Instead you'll just try to make choices that will not create a problem.

If you want to change that, you have to ask a question and make some choices. And you're not going to know what those choices will create until you choose them. If you are trying to choose a "good" choice or a "right" choice or a choice that's going to get you what you want, your choices ain't going to lead you beyond what anybody else could imagine.

You have to ask: "What choice can I make regardless of how it turns out?" I know my choices will turn out great for me because I don't choose crap. Do you choose crap?

If you don't like crap, you're not going to choose that which is going to create crap in your life. Please recognize that you've never created the crappy life that other people think is just fine. The willingness to be in question gives you choices other people don't have. It makes things possible that are not possible for other people. Ask:

- What can I choose here that I haven't chosen yet?
- If I chose this, what would life be like?"

The choice you have that others don't have has to do with choosing for you. Please look at this, folks. Have you chosen that which will create something greater in your life? Always make the choice to seek something greater. When you're seeking something greater, you can't actually make a mistake. Don't look for the mistake you made; look at the possibility you created.

WHAT CHOICE DID I MAKE THAT CREATED THIS RESULT?

Call Participant: Do we have to acknowledge all the places where we chose things that didn't work out?

Gary: Yes. Ask: "What choice did I make that created this result?" Then you say: "That was not a good choice. This is not where I want to be. I'm going to destroy and uncreate that choice and make a new one."

Call Participant: So you acknowledge that you made a choice, it didn't work out the way you wanted it to, and you make another choice? Do you just keep on choosing and acknowledging? Are you acknowledging what you know and that you're aware? Are you acknowledging your good choices and your not-so-good choices—all of that?

Gary: Yes, and you also ask: "What choices did I make that created the good parts of my life?"

Call Participant: I've made choices that didn't turn out the way I wanted them to, but I've also made choices that did turn out…

Gary: Sometimes you have to choose what isn't going to work out the way you want in order to find what you really want to choose, like I did with the house I could have made money on. I got that I didn't want to own a house like that. It wasn't pretty enough to make me proud. I wouldn't have had pride of ownership.

ACKNOWLEDGING WHAT IS WITHOUT JUDGMENT

Call Participant: Can you talk some more about acknowledgment and how to acknowledge something correctly?

Gary: It's not about acknowledging something *correctly*. It's about acknowledging *what is*. When you're looking for the *correct* acknowledgment, you're looking for how to get it right, and when you're trying to get something right, you're choosing to judge. You choose that which is wrong in order to judge the rightness or wrongness of things. It's a choice for judgment.

How many choices for judgment are you using to avoid the acknowledgment of you that you could be choosing? Everything that is times

a godzillion, will you destroy and uncreate it all? Right and Wrong,
Good and Bad, POD and POC, All 9, Shorts, Boys, and Beyonds.

Every time you choose judgment, you choose away from you
and away from acknowledgement. You have to be willing to
recognize what you're creating by the choices you're making.
By your choice alone do you create. What would happen if you
were willing to see that every choice you make creates? Most
of the time, you don't see that.

How many choices for judgment are you using to avoid the acknowl-
edgment of you that you could be choosing? Everything that is times
a godzillion, will you destroy and uncreate it all? Right and Wrong,
Good and Bad, POD and POC, All 9, Shorts, Boys, and Beyonds.

Call Participant: So you go down the road and choose the
possibility of something, then you look at it and say, "No, this
doesn't look good." You acknowledge that and then choose
again. Is that right?

Gary: Yes. When Dain and I were looking for a house in Houston, I would look at a house and say, "Wow, great lot, interesting house. This could turn out well," and then I'd say, "Yeah, but
I don't really care about it." If I don't care about something, am
I going to create something great? No. If you don't care about
it, you're not going to create with it. Every choice creates that
place, and then you choose what you care about. Every choice
means more possibilities for you to choose things that you care
about until your whole life is about caring about you.

Call Participant: So if we want to buy a house, we should look
at what we're interested in, what we like, and what gives us
joy?

Gary: Yes. Ask: "What is going to be a fun place for me to live?" When Dain and I were shopping for a house, we walked into a spacious house that had giant windows overlooking a huge porch, and we said, "Yes!" We had looked at other houses that were "nicer" and more "finished," but they didn't have the space we wanted.

Dain and I like a sense of space, so we chose based on the space of this house. Did we have to do a lot of work? Yes. Does it matter? No, because we have this thing about space.

Today while Dain and I were talking, we decided we need to change our money flows. We asked, "What would be a great way of changing the money flows here?"

I asked, "Why don't we make it our target to buy the house next door, tear it down and keep the swimming pool? We don't like the house, and we don't like the people who live in it. We could keep the swimming pool and create a wading pool for kids, and we could have a big lot with lots of pretty trees. Then we could buy the house on the other side and put up an eight-car garage. We could have two acres. That would be really fun!" What if you were willing to ask: "Wow, what could I create if I was willing to tear down the house next door?"

DO WHAT MAKES YOU HAPPY

Call Participant: Is that where happiness is just a choice—if it makes you happy?

Gary: If you do what makes you happy, everything in life tends to be that which creates happiness and joy and possibility. Look at that and see how it works for you. Create what you've already created and ask for more.

We'll end with: Do what makes you happy and then everything in life tends to be that which creates happiness and joy and possibility.

THE FIRST CALL

CLEARINGS

How many choices are you using to create the right and wrong of this reality as the only choice, the no choice universe you are choosing? Everything that is times a godzillion, will you destroy and uncreate it all? Right and Wrong, Good and Bad, POD and POC, All 9, Shorts, Boys, and Beyonds.

What choices did you make that created the reality about you and your money you do not desire, like, or are happy with? Everything that is times a godzillion, will you destroy and uncreate it all? Right and Wrong, Good and Bad, POD and POC, All 9, Shorts, Boys, and Beyonds.

What have you been unwilling to see, do, perceive, know, be, and receive about the choices you make that keep you from having everything you could have, will you destroy and uncreate all that? Right and Wrong, Good and Bad, POD and POC, All 9, Shorts, Boys, and Beyonds.

What possibilities are you refusing that you really could be choosing that if you would choose them would create a different reality for you in every aspect of your life? Everything that is times a godzillion, will you destroy and uncreate it all? Right and Wrong, Good and Bad, POD and POC, All 9, Shorts, Boys, and Beyonds.

What can nobody else choose that you have never acknowledged you can choose that if you acknowledged you could choose it would change reality with every choice you make? Everything that is times a godzillion, will you destroy and uncreate it all? Right and Wrong, Good and Bad, POD and POC, All 9, Shorts, Boys, and Beyonds.

How many choices for judgment are you using to avoid the acknowledgment of you that you could be choosing? Everything that is times a godzillion, will you destroy and uncreate it all? Right and Wrong, Good and Bad, POD and POC, All 9, Shorts, Boys, and Beyonds.

THE SECOND CALL

Learning How to Choose

You need to ask a question in order to know what to choose.

Gary: Hello, everyone. Welcome to our second call. Let's start with a question.

CHOOSING WITHOUT PROJECTION OR EXPECTATION

Call Participant: It seems like I've misunderstood choice as a conclusion or a decision that leads to judgment and expectation. Could I make a choice to actualize something instantly?

Gary: When you choose without a projection or expectation, the things that you choose actualize more and more quickly.

Call Participant: So should I list all the choices I would like to make?

Gary: Most people have a tendency to choose something and then decide, conclude, and judge, "Well now, that's a good choice." That's not what I'm talking about. Those are not *choices*; those are *conclusions* about what you should choose.

That is completely different from the awareness that comes from saying: "Okay, I've got ten seconds to choose the rest of my life. What would I like to choose?"

You need to choose in ten-second increments. Choosing in ten-second increments is: "I've got ten seconds to choose the rest of my life. What would I choose?" Do that and then ask: "What else would I choose?" When you start to choose in ten-second increments, you are learning how to choose. Choice does not come automatically; it comes with a price called awareness.

What have you made so vital about the rightness and wrongness of choice that keeps you from choosing that which will complement and create a reality that is actualized based on your choices? Everything that is times a godzillion, will you destroy and uncreate it all? Right and Wrong, Good and Bad, POD and POC, All 9, Shorts, Boys, and Beyonds.

And again:

What have you made so vital about the rightness and wrongness of choice that keeps you from choosing that which will complement and create a reality that is actualized based on your choices? Everything that is times a godzillion, will you destroy and uncreate it all? Right and Wrong, Good and Bad, POD and POC, All 9, Shorts, Boys, and Beyonds.

What have you made so vital about the rightness and wrongness of choice that keeps you from choosing that which will complement and create a reality that is actualized based on your choices? Everything that is times a godzillion, will you destroy and uncreate it all? Right and Wrong, Good and Bad, POD and POC, All 9, Shorts, Boys, and Beyonds.

DO YOU CHOOSE NOT TO CHOOSE?

Call Participant: I have more awareness now, and I see that way more is possible. There is much more choice and many of those choices could create something greater, but I don't know how to choose.

Gary: Is it true that you don't know how to choose? Or do you choose not to choose? Is that actually your choice?

Call Participant: Yes, I choose not to choose.

Gary: When all choices are available, not choosing is one of the choices you have. You can make yourself wrong if you don't choose the choices you could choose because you don't want to make a choice, because if you made a choice then you might be wrong, and you don't really want to be wrong but you don't mind being wrong as long as nobody else knows you're wrong. So those are choices you will always make!

What have you made so vital about the rightness and wrongness of choice that keeps you from choosing that which will complement and create a reality that is actualized based on your reality? Everything that is times a godzillion, will you destroy and uncreate it all? Right and Wrong, Good and Bad, POD and POC, All 9, Shorts, Boys, and Beyonds.

Do you get that you don't really want to choose your reality? You think that if you choose somebody else's reality, it's a better choice. Everything that brought up and let down, will you destroy and uncreate it all? Right and Wrong, Good and Bad, POD and POC, All 9, Shorts, Boys, and Beyonds.

ARE YOU GOING TO CHOOSE YOUR TRUE DESIRE?

Call Participant: What questions can I ask to generate bigger, greater, and faster possibilities for my life and living, money, sex, relationship, happiness, and joy?

Gary: Are money, sex, relationship, happiness, and joy your true desires for your life and living? Or do you desire something greater than that?

If you don't get what your true desire is, you create a place where you're wrong for any choice outside of things like money, sex, and relationship, because that's what you're supposed to choose according to this reality. Are you going to choose according to this reality, because that's the reality you've got? Or are you going to choose your true desire?

Call Participant: Yeah, I get that it's totally different when you can trust and know that you don't have to choose things that are specific to this reality, like sex and money, and that you can have all those things—and you can keep choosing what has never existed before.

CHOOSING BEYOND ANYBODY'S CAPACITY TO STOP YOU

Call Participant: Is there a clearing we can do to create and generate greater possibility with choice?

Gary: What energy, space, and consciousness can I be to create a royal capacity for choosing and possibility beyond anybody else's capacity to stop me can I be? Everything that doesn't allow that, times a godzillion, will you destroy and uncreate it all? Right and Wrong, Good and Bad, POD and POC, All 9, Shorts, Boys and Beyonds.

Call Participant: Would you talk some more about the part of the clearing where you mentioned creating beyond anybody's capacity to stop us?

Gary: Do you get that in this reality you're always looking for who can stop you?

Freedom is being unstoppable.

Call Participant: What's required to change that?

Gary: Choice. It's: "Nobody is ever going to stop me. Nobody's ever going to keep me from choosing what I want to choose." You might want to watch the movie, *The Unsinkable Molly Brown,* and become her. The Debbie Reynolds musical version would be right up your alley.

What energy, space, and consciousness can I be to create a royal capacity for choosing and possibility beyond anybody else's capacity to stop me can I be? Everything that doesn't allow that times a godzillion, will you destroy and uncreate it all? Right and Wrong, Good and Bad, POD and POC, All 9, Shorts, Boys, and Beyonds.

Call Participant: Is it the willingness to make my choice greater than anybody else's choice?

Gary: It's the willingness to realize that your choice for you is going to be greater than anybody else's choice for you could ever be. Have you tried to make your parents' choice for you right?

Call Participant: Yes.

Gary: Did that work for you?

Call Participant: No.

Gary: Are you your parents?

Call Participant: No.

Gary: Are you a conglomeration of what they are?

Call Participant: No!

Gary: Right, you're not, but you keep trying to act like they somehow have the influence and the desire to save you from yourself and that they want you to be everything you can be. Is that true and real or a lie?

Call Participant: That's a lie.

Gary: Everything you've done to become what your parents want you to be, will you destroy and uncreate all that? Right and Wrong, Good and Bad, POD and POC, All 9, Shorts, Boys, and Beyonds.

And everywhere you've tried to be a conglomeration of who your parents are, will you destroy and uncreate all that? Right and Wrong, Good and Bad, POD and POC, All 9, Shorts, Boys, and Beyonds.

You can't be a conglomeration of your parents or anyone else. You've got to choose to be what works for you. Let's try this clearing one more time.

What energy, space, and consciousness can I be to create a royal capacity for choosing and possibility beyond anybody else's capacity to stop me can I be? Everything that doesn't allow that times a godzillion, will you destroy and uncreate it all? Right and Wrong, Good and Bad, POD and POC, All 9, Shorts, Boys, and Beyonds.

Call Participant: I recognize that I've chosen my husband's judgments and choices rather than acknowledging me and my greatness. I'd like to change this.

Gary: You can't, because if you did, you'd have to give up your husband! No, you wouldn't—but you'd have to give up your husband's judgment as true for you.

Everything you've done to buy your husband's judgment, or anybody else's judgment, as true for you—your husband, your wife, your family, your significant other, your stupid other, the other that you're stupid with, whatever—will you destroy and uncreate all that? Right and Wrong, Good and Bad, POD and POC, All 9, Shorts, Boys, and Beyonds.

Everything you've done to buy your husband's judgment, or anybody else's judgment, as true for you—your husband, your wife, your family, your significant other, your stupid other, the other that you're stupid with, whatever—will you destroy and uncreate all that? Right and Wrong, Good and Bad, POD and POC, All 9, Shorts, Boys, and Beyonds.

CREATING A REALITY BEYOND THIS REALITY WITH TOTAL EASE

Call Participant: I'm willing to have my reality and to care for and nurture my body and me. I'm willing to create more for my life and future reality. What do I institute today to create oneness and to have that show up with total ease?

Gary: What energy, space, and consciousness can my body and I be that allows me to create a reality beyond this reality with total ease? Everything that doesn't allow that to show up times a godzillion, will you destroy and uncreate it all? Right and Wrong, Good and Bad, POD and POC, All 9, Shorts, Boys, and Beyonds.

Call Participant: What can I let go of today to create a greater tomorrow for my future reality? What am I not willing to acknowledge and let go of?

Gary: What future have you created and are you aware of that you have not acknowledged is actualizing with the rapidity that outstretches and fights this reality that if you acknowledged it would create a sense of peace and ease and total possibility for all eternity? Everything that is times a godzillion, will you destroy and uncreate it all? Right and Wrong, Good and Bad, POD and POC, All 9, Shorts, Boys, and Beyonds.

Most of you have started to choose for you, for the first time in your life.

Once you start choosing for you, you begin to actualize a reality that fights this reality.

What future have you created and are you aware of that you have not acknowledged is actualizing with the rapidity that outstretches and fights this reality that if you acknowledged it would create a sense of peace and ease and total possibility for all eternity? Everything that is times a godzillion, will you destroy and uncreate it all? Right and Wrong, Good and Bad, POD and POC, All 9, Shorts, Boys, and Beyonds.

Once you recognize the choice you are not happy with, you destroy and uncreate it, you POC and POD it, you get present with it, and you acknowledge it.

THROWING A BOULDER INTO THE POND

Call Participant: As more of us begin to choose our reality, are we able to influence what's happening in the world, with things like mass killings? Does a totally different reality get created or does the reality on the planet get shifted because there are people choosing in a different way?

Gary: Ask: "What energy, space, and consciousness can I be that would change this in totality with total ease?" You can have an effect on all kinds of things. It's like throwing a boulder into a pond; the first ripple is the biggest. The second ripple is smaller, the third smaller than that, and so on. At first you will mostly affect the people in your immediate sphere of influence, and as you affect them, your influence will go out into the rest of the world.

The first sphere includes the people around you, the ones you are closest to. You become the boulder that goes in the pond and creates a big wave, which allows them to expand out beyond their level of influence, and that big wave creates another set of small waves, which creates another set of smaller waves until it becomes an influential wave in the world.

Call Participant: Is it like giving somebody a smile instead of a frown and changing their day, and then they change somebody else's day?

Gary: Exactly. It works the other way, too. The first time I went to New Zealand, I realized that New Zealand is sort of like the United States used to be prior to the book *In Cold Blood*, which was published in 1959. It is the story of two ex-convicts who murdered a Texas farm family. After that book came out, I watched people who used to greet you in the street suddenly become paranoid. That book did so much damage to everybody! It was a giant boulder that Truman Capote threw into the world. His point of view was that if you invited somebody into your home, they were going to kill you.

People had been inviting others into their homes for hundreds of years and nobody had ever been slaughtered like that. For me, the important point was not that you might get slaughtered if you invited someone into your home; the important point was to be aware of who you were inviting home.

So use this question with anything that you have a concern about: "What energy, space, and consciousness can I be to change all of this in totality, with total ease?"

Today I was on a broadcast show with a lady from Israel, and Israel now wants me to go there to do a Choice of Possibility class. I said, "Get 100 people, and I'll come. If I don't have 100 people, it's not economically viable for me. There are too many other places with over 100 people that are demanding my attention. So get at least 100 people and we'll be fine."

The lady said, "Well, people here would want that."

I said, "Cool." Had I ever heard that before? No. Why hadn't I heard it before? Because it had not become a reality until then. The boulders were thrown into the pond for a long time before that became a reality.

WHAT DOES *VORTEXING* MEAN?

Gary: You're all starting to vortex.

Call Participant: What does *vortexing* mean?

Gary: A vortex is when the energy opens up. It happens when you tap into the god source, the oneness that you actually are. It feels like a cool breeze somewhere in your body. It might feel like your shoulders are cold, or your legs are cold, or your knees are cold, or your shins are cold, or your feet in your shoes are cold. Those are all signs of a vortex. When you are vortexing, practically speaking, there is little I can do to change anything because you are in a blissed state rather than a blistered state. All of your edges become smooth and everything becomes easier.

Call Participant: I thought you said that because people were fading out; they were not present anymore.

Gary: No, they are so present that when they think about something, it starts to disappear. When you are vortexing, that's what happens. You think about something and it starts to disappear, and you no longer have a question. You keep thinking about things and they keep disappearing.

Call Participant: If we're all fried and we can't change, is that a space where we can create?

Gary: The vortex does not necessarily equal creation. It does equal a place where you could begin to actualize a possibility if you are willing to know what you want to create.

> *What have you chosen to create that you are not acknowledging as creation, that if you acknowledged it as creation would allow it to actualize exponentially? Everything that brings up and lets down, will you destroy and uncreate it all? Right and Wrong, Good and Bad, POD and POC, All 9, Shorts, Boys, and Beyonds.*

And the vortex gets bigger!

Does anyone have a question?

DRAMA VS. CREATION

Call Participant: Would you talk about what drama is? As we get into creation, there's almost a euphoria that forms. It seems like we're elated, and when drama comes into the picture, it has a lower or heavier sense. What can we call the creation, other than creation and elevation and elation?

Gary: You could call it fun!

Call Participant: (laughs) Fun. Joy. Bliss. All of those good things.

Gary: Drama is when somebody else doesn't like you having fun so they do drama to try to get you out of the fun. Isn't it cute that people don't want you to have fun? They create drama so you will choose drama instead of fun. Unfortunately, once you hit this place of the vortex, the possibility, the choice, and the freedom come in and you say, "Thanks for sharing the drama. It's such wonderful crap. You just made me realize how much more fun it is to create what I want to create instead of what you create."

Call Participant: (laughs) Thank you. I knew that there was a high and a low there.

Gary: The high is you and the low is everybody else. It's just a choice you have to make.

HOMEPLAY

Gary: Well, I've taken you as far as I can take you at this moment. I'd love to say I could do more today, but I can't. Hopefully we can take it further on the next call. It's going to depend on your choices—on what you choose.

I'm going to give you something to do before the next call so we can have you a little bit more caved in and miserable. I want you to run: "What energy, space, and consciousness can I be to avoid the gift of me for all eternity?" That's your homeplay.

Call Participant: And we're running this why?

Gary: Because of all the stuff that will come up that we can erase, which will be fun!

THE SECOND CALL

CLEARINGS

What have you made so vital about the rightness and wrongness of choice that keeps you from choosing that which will complement and create a reality that is actualized based on your choices? Everything that is times a godzillion, will you destroy and uncreate it all? Right and Wrong, Good and Bad, POD and POC, All 9, Shorts, Boys, and Beyonds.

Do you get that you don't really want to choose your reality? You think that if you choose somebody else's reality it's a better choice. Everything that brought up, will you destroy and uncreate it all? Right and Wrong, Good and Bad, POD and POC, All 9, Shorts, Boys, and Beyonds.

What energy, space, and consciousness can I be to create a royal capacity for choosing and possibility beyond anybody else's capacity to stop me can I be? Everything that doesn't allow that, times a godzillion, will you destroy and uncreate it all? Right and Wrong, Good and Bad, POD and POC, All 9, Shorts, Boys and Beyonds.

Everything you've done to become what your parents want you to be, will you destroy and uncreate all that? Right and Wrong, Good and Bad, POD and POC, All 9, Shorts, Boys, and Beyonds.

And everywhere you've tried to be a conglomeration of who your parents are, will you destroy and uncreate all that? Right and Wrong, Good and Bad, POD and POC, All 9, Shorts, Boys, and Beyonds.

Everything you've done to buy your husband's judgment, or any-body else's judgment, as true for you—your husband, your wife, your family, your significant other, your stupid other, the other that you're stupid with, whatever—will you destroy and uncreate all that? Right and Wrong, Good and Bad, POD and POC, All 9, Shorts, Boys, and Beyonds.

What energy, space, and consciousness can my body and I be that allows me to create a reality beyond this reality with total ease? Everything that doesn't allow that to show up times a godzillion, will you destroy and uncreate it all? Right and Wrong, Good and Bad, POD and POC, All 9, Shorts, Boys, and Beyonds.

What future have you created and are you aware of that you have not acknowledged is actualizing with the rapidity that outstretches and fights this reality that if you acknowledged it would create a sense of peace and ease and total possibility for all eternity? Every-thing that is times a godzillion, will you destroy and uncreate it all? Right and Wrong, Good and Bad, POD and POC, All 9, Shorts, Boys, and Beyonds.

What have you chosen to create that you are not acknowledging as creation, that if you acknowledged it as creation would allow it to actualize exponentially? Everything that brings up and lets down, will you destroy and uncreate it all? Right and Wrong, Good and Bad, POD and POC, All 9, Shorts, Boys, and Beyonds.

THE THIRD CALL

Living from Possibilities

You need to choose in order to
see what's possible.

If you could choose anything,
what would you choose?

Would you choose to be right?

Would you choose to be wrong?

Or would you choose to have total
choice and infinite possibilities?

CHOICE AND FREEDOM

Gary: Hello, everyone. Let's start with a question.

Call Participant: If I'm aware that I'm not willing to choose or be free, what can I run in order to have the willingness to create choice and freedom as something that's fun rather than something to be judged or penalized for?

Gary: What have you made so vital about choosing penalties that keeps you always choosing that which will penalize you and never being the possibilities and the freedom that possibilities bring? Everything that is times a godzillion, will you destroy and uncreate it all? Right and Wrong, Good and Bad, POD and POC, All 9, Shorts, Boys, and Beyonds.

Let's run that again:

> *What have you made so vital about choosing penalties that keeps you always choosing that which will penalize you and never being the possibilities and the freedom that possibilities bring? Everything that is times a godzillion, will you destroy and uncreate it all? Right and Wrong, Good and Bad, POD and POC, All 9, Shorts, Boys, and Beyonds.*

You come into this life with an innate capacity to choose; therefore, you have freedom. But you give away your freedom in the need to live in other people's realities, or the need to believe that other people have a reality that's greater than yours, or the need to believe that your needs equal a place that you have to choose from. You believe you have to choose *from your needs* rather than *to your desires and your possibilities.*

What have you made so vital about never choosing for, through, by, and with possibility that keeps you seeking right or wrong as the reason and justification for every choice you choose? Everything that is times a godzillion, will you destroy and uncreate it all? Right and Wrong, Good and Bad, POD and POC, All 9, Shorts, Boys, and Beyonds.

What have you made so vital about never choosing for, through, by, and with possibility that keeps you seeking right or wrong as the reason and justification for every choice you choose? Everything that is times a godzillion, will you destroy and uncreate it all? Right and Wrong, Good and Bad, POD and POC, All 9, Shorts, Boys, and Beyonds.

Call Participant: If you choose without judgment, are you choosing for, through, by, and with possibility?

Gary: Yes. And every time there's a judgment, you're locked into rightness or wrongness, and you will give up.

What have you made so vital about never choosing for, through, by, and with possibility that keeps you seeking right or wrong as the reason and justification for every choice you choose? Everything that is times a godzillion, will you destroy and uncreate it all? Right and Wrong, Good and Bad, POD and POC, All 9, Shorts, Boys, and Beyonds.

You try to avoid being wrong by choosing rightly, and when that doesn't work out, you believe you chose wrong; therefore, everything you thought was right actually isn't right. It's wrong, and you're really screwed up because you've never chosen the right choice in your entire life!

Everything that brought up and let down, will you destroy and un-create it all? Right and Wrong, Good and Bad, POD and POC, All 9, Shorts, Boys, and Beyonds.

JUDGMENT LIMITS WHAT IS POSSIBLE

Gary: Each of us has chosen continuously for our thousands of lifetimes, and we have made choices in those lifetimes that have created the possibilities that show up in this lifetime. However, if you judge what shows up in your lifetime instead of going to the question and saying: "I wonder what's possible now," you start limiting what's possible.

You make your judgment the reason for not having in this lifetime. That's why the idea of karma is such an un-delightful thing. "My karma made me do that." No, it wasn't your karma. It was a choice you made in some other lifetime that is showing up now in order to get cleared away, which means what? It means nothing. It means it showed up. The question is: "Now, what would I like to choose from here?"

How many choices do you have from other lifetimes that are determining what you will not be, do, have, create, and generate this lifetime? You have made a whole lot of choices in past lives that are frigging stupid! But instead of making a different choice this lifetime, you try to make right what you chose in the past so you can prove you didn't make a wrong choice. How's that working for you?

What have you made so vital about never choosing for, through, by, and with possibility that keeps you seeking right or wrong as the reason and justification for every choice you choose or have chosen in all lifetimes? Everything that is times a godzillion, will you destroy

and uncreate it all? Right and Wrong, Good and Bad, POD and POC,
All 9, Shorts, Boys, and Beyonds.

CHOOSING WITH A POSSIBILITY POINT OF VIEW

Call Participant: What is an example of choosing with possibility?

Gary: I recently had a chance to buy a set of African art. I went to look at it and thought, "Oh, my God, this is amazing, this is beautiful, this is fabulous." The art spoke to me. I asked it, "Are you full of possibilities?" and it said, "Yes."

I told the guy who was selling the art, "I want to buy it. How much do you want for it?" He said, "$150,000."

I went to Dain and said, "I don't have $150,000. Do you want to invest in this art with me?" Dain went to see it and said, "Yes," so we bought it.

What's really possible in the way you spend your money? Are you are trying to figure out whether you're spending your money from a right or wrong point of view rather than a possibility point of view?

Call Participant: Can you say more about spending your money with a possibility point of view?

Gary: Have you ever bought a house or a car? Did you do it because you thought it was a good investment or because you could see a possibility and something greater showing up because of it?

Call Participant: I've always bought a house based on what I can improve about it.

Gary: That's based on possibility.

Call Participant: But it hasn't seemed like I've created possibilities.

Gary: That's because you determined and decided you had to do it from an investment point of view. You could only buy it if you decided it was a good investment. I've tried to get you to choose possibility because I haven't seen you choosing possibility. You don't choose from the point of view: "What can I create with this?"

Call Participant: When we choose possibility from the energy of something, do we molecularly change the energy as we are choosing?

Gary: Yes. Every choice creates. Have you ever heard of Feng Shui? You arrange the things in your space in a particular order so you can obtain a particular energy that makes it a more valuable and better place to live. I don't do Feng Shui by the "design" point of view; I do Feng Shui based on these questions:

- How does this create a different energy here?
- If I add this thing, what does that do?
- If I change this and put it here, does it change anything?

If I put one thing here and another thing there, does it change something? Yes, it does. And with that change, what am I doing? I'm creating and changing things for the joy of it and because it creates an energy that works for me.

Use these questions to see the energies of a different possibility than anybody else has the ability to create:

- What is this choice going to create?
- If I choose this, what will my life be like in five years?
- If I don't choose this what will my life be like in five years?
- If I choose to create this, what will the world be like in twenty-five years? Fifty years? A hundred years? Five hundred years?

Call Participant: Can my choice create a reality beyond this reality even though right now I'm still struggling to believe that it's possible? Can I still go ahead and make choices?

Gary: Your choice is to believe that you're struggling to believe you have choice. Maybe you could just acknowledge the fact and ask: "When have I chosen so badly that I haven't been able to create greater?"

WHO DOES THIS BELONG TO?

Call Participant: I have a habit of choosing limitation instead of possibility. For example, I should have gone to bed earlier last night because I had to get up at three a.m. to be on this call. But I was having so much fun that I chose against my health.

Gary: That's a judgment and not a reality. How did you get to the point of view that you had a problem with getting up at three a.m.?

Call Participant: I suppose it was because I woke up tired. But then, you would be tired at three a.m., wouldn't you?

Gary: I'm sorry, were *you* tired at three a.m.? Or were there a lot of *tired people* who got up at three a.m.? Who did the tiredness belong to?[2]

Call Participant: Ohhh! Yeah.

Gary: Are you aware of other people's tiredness?

Call Participant: Yeah, right! Thank you.

Gary: Oh my goodness, you're aware!

Call Participant: You get it when you get it, right?

Gary: Yeah. You get it when you get it and you don't get it until you get it. That's the way it works.

ACKNOWLEDGE THE FUTURE YOU'VE CHOSEN

Call Participant: Sometimes I am aware of the future from an energetic perspective. How do I choose that? Or do I need to...

Gary: Whoa. Whoa. Whoa. You've already chosen that future by being willing to see it. So now you have to ask: "What do I need to be or do today to bring that to fruition right away?"

Call Participant: Do I have to say, "right away?" Sometimes things take a really long time to come to fruition. It can be years.

---

2 "Who does this belong to?" is an Access Consciousness tool you can use if you're interested in having more fun and joy in your life. That's because ninety-eight percent of the thoughts, feelings, and emotions you have are not even yours. You can find out more about this at: http://access-consciousness-blog.com/2015/10/are-you-an-empath-or-are-you-aware/ or at: https://www.youtube.com/watch?v=CI6TULGyOrY

Gary: Yes, but, "right away" can be ten years, because your capacity to create and be aware doesn't fit this reality's dogmatic approach to time.

Call Participant: How can I be more patient? Sometimes I get bored of something if it takes a really long time.

Gary: There's something you have to understand about the question: "What can I be or do different today to bring this to fruition right away?" You just have to acknowledge the future you've chosen. You just have to acknowledge it. You don't have to put 800 pounds of attention on it. Put ten seconds of attention on it once a day, nothing more.

Are you creating it and not acknowledging it, and in the process of not acknowledging it, are you undoing everything you're creating?

Call Participant: Oh! Sometimes, yes.

Gary: You undo it when you start judging it, you undo it when you think it's not happening, you undo it when you say you're not patient.

YOUR ENERGY IS A CONTRIBUTION

Call Participant: Do you undo it when you don't acknowledge it and you think it's not a big deal? Sometimes something will show up and I'll just say, "Oh yeah."

Gary: You have to recognize that your energy is a contribution. For example, Dain and I are a contribution to the plants and animals at our house in a way that few other people are, and as a result, we have more animals and more unique plants than anyone else does. We have things growing at our house that shouldn't be growing at this time of year. All kinds of things happen and people ask, "How do you do that?" It's because we contribute to everything and everything contributes back. It's question, choice, possibility, and contribution.

So when you perceive the future, you recognize, "Oh! That's the future." Then you ask: "What do I need to be or do different today to bring this to fruition right away?" Your idea of "right away" is "Why didn't it happen yesterday?"

Call Participant: That's right! Actually, last week!

Gary: That's my point of view, too. But if you know that you're going to contribute to it whatever you can, when you can, when you can receive it, when it can be a contribution, all kinds of other possibilities and opportunities show up for you as a result of the willingness to be in contribution to the future that you know can be.

The ability to be aware of the future is a gift you have, but you think it is a curse because you don't know how to institute it to make it happen the way you think it's supposed to happen. You have to ask:

- What can I be or do to create this more rapidly?
- What can I be or do different to bring this to fruition right away?
- What can I be or do to create a possibility that I have never considered?

THE JOY OF ACTUALIZING THINGS

Call Participant: Can I ask you about the rapidity thing? I have a love/hate relationship with it. You know how fast I am and how much I love that about myself, and yet there's always a slight twist in it for me, especially with my body.

Gary: What is the thing you're having a problem with—or *thinking* you're having a problem with? By the way, it's mostly *thinking* you're having a problem with it.

Call Participant: My body freaks out when we go too fast, and yet I love it at the same time.

Gary: No, your *body* does not freak out. Your body is like a little kid when it gets excited. It jumps up and down and says, "Oh, goody!" It's more like *you* don't want to have the speed you had as a kid, do you?

Call Participant: I don't remember being fast as a kid.

Gary: I know, but fast for you is not what fast is for everybody else.

Call Participant: That's true.

Gary: Did you ever get accused of bouncing off the walls?

Call Participant: No, actually. I was a very quiet child. For me it has always been my energy and my brain that have been fast, not my body.

Gary: I think your body has been as fast as your energy and your brain, but you were trying to delude everybody into thinking that you were a calm, cool, and collected person, knowing that capacity would give you more credence in the world than other things.

Call Participant: Oh.

Gary: That was not awareness of the future, was it?

Call Participant: Well, I'm going to say *yes*. I don't actually get it, but I'll just say *yes*.

Gary: You're standing in an affirmative *yes*. It doesn't make sense the way you want it to make sense, but that's what it is.

Call Participant: What's it coming from when my body gets uncomfortable? What is the discomfort? I'm confused.

Gary: What have you not acknowledged?

Call Participant: Oh, it's a not acknowledging?

Gary: Yeah.

What future are you actualizing that you're not acknowledging? Everything that is times a godzillion, will you destroy and uncreate it all? Right and Wrong, Good and Bad, POD and POC, All 9, Shorts, Boys, and Beyonds.

Call Participant: What do I do with that? That's where I get freaked out.

Gary: First of all, you've got to stop saying that you're getting "freaked out," because you're not! There's a level of happiness in knowing you're bringing things to fruition that you knew could come to fruition!

Call Participant: Why does it make me cry, then?

Gary: Because your body is grateful for the fact that it's being acknowledged! You've been invalidating your body your whole life. Your body's saying, "Thank God!"

Call Participant: Oh, right! (sighs) (laughs) I get it.

Gary: Notice that sigh?

Call Participant: Yeah.

Gary: How does your body feel?

Call Participant: Better. It's getting more space.

Gary: Okay, so your body likes having space. Do you?

Call Participant: Yeah.

Gary: Then why do you always contract when you feel that sense of possibility of space?

Call Participant: I didn't realize I was contracting.

Gary: "I am freaking out" is contraction. It's not the question: "What the hell is this and what do I do with it?"

Call Participant: So when my body gets like jelly, what is that?

Gary: Fun. Relaxation. Rest.

Call Participant: Oh! Okay!

Gary: Be careful. It might turn out better than you think!

IS *LACK* A REALITY OR A CONCLUSION?

Call Participant: Could you please speak to the energy of "If I spend this money, it'll be gone"? It's the idea that there is a lack or that I will use it all up.

Gary: Is that a reality or a conclusion?

Call Participant: It is a conclusion.

Gary: Does it allow you to have choice? Or is that someone else's reality that you're trying to project and expect into existence?

Call Participant: It's someone else's.

Gary: The good part about this is that you can make yourself into a pile of shit really easily. That's got to be better than choosing what's good for you, isn't it?

Call Participant: Instant judgment. All you have to do is not choose for you!

Gary: We're going to have a sale on instant judgment. For $5.95 you can get 800 judgments.

Call Participant: Can you talk about *need* and what that has to do with choice?

Gary: Most people function from the point of view that they *need* something. They create their lives based on their needs; for example, "I need a new car, therefore I have to do blah, blah, blah." You have no need. You could choose to have anything you wanted just because you want it.

WHAT DO YOU WANT TO CREATE?

Call Participant: When I ask, "What would I like my life to be like?" everything seems cloudy. What is that?

Gary: It seems cloudy because you have no clarity. Run: "What energy, space, and consciousness can I be to have total clarity and ease with everything I desire to create that I've never been aware of for all eternity?" You haven't chosen and now you're saying, "What do I want to choose? I have no clue!" You have to start using ten-second increments of choice. In every ten seconds of choice, you have a different possibility. Ask:

- What do I have awareness of that other people don't?
- How can I use this to create and generate a life that will be fun for me?"

You've never created your life for fun, have you?

Call Participant: At times I have.

Gary: At times. That's like saying, "Occasionally happiness breaks out in my life."

Call Participant: That's exactly how it has been!

Gary: That's not creating your life. That's having something happen to you. This is the place where you have to ask: "What can I create or generate here that I haven't considered?" It's something you choose.

Choice happens with no effort, but unlike breathing, which you do whether or not you're conscious of it, choice is done from a conscious state. You have to remind yourself to choose every ten seconds.

Call Participant: What exercise can I use to train myself to do that?

Gary: Go outside, and when you have no sense that you need to do anything, when you have no desire to do anything and you can just sit in your chair and do nothing forever, get the idea that you're going to die in the next ten seconds, and say: "I've got ten seconds to create the rest of my life."

What would you like to have on your tombstone when they bury you? Write your epitaph. Is it: "I lived a life where I didn't have any problems but I didn't have much fun. Occasionally I had fun and that was kind of cool"? Is that good enough for you? Or do you want something different? What do you want to create?

FEAR IS A LIE YOU BUY TO LIMIT WHAT YOU CHOOSE

Call Participant: I have a tendency to go backward, to what is known instead of forward, to an unknown space. There is a fear of stepping into a world of constantly choosing.

Gary: Bullshit! You wouldn't even be able to make that statement if you had any fear. Fear is a lie you buy in order to limit what you choose!

All the fear you bought as true in order to limit you, will you destroy and uncreate all that? Right and Wrong, Good and Bad, POD and POC, All 9, Shorts, Boys, and Beyonds.

What fear are you using to create the limitations of what you can choose are you choosing? Everything that is times a godzillion, will you destroy and uncreate it all? Right and Wrong, Good and Bad, POD and POC, All 9, Shorts, Boys, and Beyonds.

You have no fear. Get over the idea that fear is real. Stop buying other people's projections and expectations about what's real.

All the fear you bought as true in order to limit you, will you destroy and uncreate all that? Right and Wrong, Good and Bad, POD and POC, All 9, Shorts, Boys, and Beyonds.

CHOOSING TO PERCEIVE, KNOW, BE, AND RECEIVE

Call Participant: You've said that choice is innate to us. How do perception, knowing, being, and receiving fit into this? Are they innate as well? Or do we have to choose to perceive, know, be, and receive?

Gary: It's a choice to perceive, know, be, and receive. You have the *ability* to perceive, know, be, and receive, but *choice* is what creates those as something greater. How many choices have you made not to be aware?

Call Participant: Lots, but that's changing.

Gary: It's changing because you're choosing to say, "Wait a minute, I'd rather be aware than think all this is going to be fine."

How many choices have you chosen to avoid the knowing you could have all the time? Everything that is times a godzillion, will you destroy and uncreate it all? Right and Wrong, Good and Bad, POD and POC, All 9, Shorts, Boys, and Beyonds.

How many choices have you made not to be, so you can live in this do-do reality? Everything that is times a godzillion, will you destroy and uncreate it all? Right and Wrong, Good and Bad, POD and POC, All 9, Shorts, Boys, and Beyonds.

How many choices have you made not to perceive in order to make sure that you don't have to have total awareness? Everything that is times a godzillion, will you destroy and uncreate it all? Right and Wrong, Good and Bad, POD and POC, All 9, Shorts, Boys, and Beyonds.

How many choices have you made not to receive to make sure you get to struggle through this reality? Everything that is times a godzillion, will you destroy and uncreate it all? Right and Wrong, Good and Bad, POD and POC, All 9, Shorts, Boys, and Beyonds.

WHAT DO YOU LOVE ABOUT YOUR LIFE?

Call Participant: I see that I've had a great life and that I don't acknowledge it.

Gary: You've got to acknowledge what you've got or you can't create beyond it.

Call Participant: Can you give me some tips on how to get better at that?

Gary: Like every other stupid person on the planet, you don't look at what you love about your life; you look for what's wrong with it. You need to get up every morning and say, "I love my life!" then look around and ask:

- What do I love about my life?
- What do I love about my house?
- What do I love about my children?
- What do I love about my partner?
- What do I love about everything I get to do and everything I get to be?'

Call Participant: Thank you. It's so simple.

Gary: It is simple, yet we keep trying to make it hard.

Call Participant: This year I've come to the space where I can choose anything. I can do pretty much anything. There are so many possibilities. I'm not asking for a definition of how to choose, but I want to know where can I put my energy to create the greatest? How do I get to that space?

Gary: Use the question I just gave you: "What do I love about my life?" When you get a sense of gratitude for the life you've created, you can create more. If you don't acknowledge that what you've created is great, all you can look for is what's wrong.

Love your life totally. Look at what you love about your life. What do you love about the family you chose? I wake up in the morning and I say, "I love my life! I have amazing people in my life, everywhere, all the time. I feel so fortunate."

I ask, "Wow! What did I do to deserve all this?" Do I have an answer? No, but I know it has a lot to do with the sex, drugs, and rock and roll that I used to do all the time! I used to think that the best thing in life was to be a rebel. Being a rebel meant I had to be an outlaw. Being an outlaw meant I had to break all the rules, and being able to break all the rules and not get caught meant I was frigging smart, which meant I was really a crappy criminal, because criminals always get caught. I did all kinds of wild, wacky, crazy and over-the-top stuff, but I never got caught. Why? Because it was not my reality that I would be caught. It was not my reality I would go to jail. And the one time I did get caught, I turned my life around totally.

WHAT WOULD YOU REALLY LIKE TO CHOOSE NOW?

Call Participant: Are you saying I need to be naughtier?

Gary: You need to get that you didn't bother to create being rebellious and breaking the rules because your point of view was: "I'm going to have what I want, the way I want it, when I want it, so there!

Call Participant: Yes, when I was young, I was very clear about that.

Gary: Why do you say that as though it's past tense? Why isn't it "Oh, this is what I am and this is the way it is"?

You've got to have a different possibility and a different reality. Why? Because you can! You keep looking for a reason and justification for choosing what you choose. That's causal reality. Instead why not say, "I don't have to live like anybody else!" Living from possibilities is the freedom of knowing you always have more choices and asking: "What would I really like to choose now?"

Call Participant: I am choosing a lot. Everything I am choosing now is making me happy. And I know there's more.

Gary: You know there's more, and the way to get it is by talking about how much you love your life and the things you love in your life. It's called having gratitude for everything you have and everything you are and everything that shows up in your life.

If you look at the universe, it's clear that each thing is inter-connected with every other thing. Please start looking at what you love about your life, because if you acknowledge what you have created, you acknowledge the quantum entanglements, and they will say, "Oh, you want more of that? No problem! Let us help you."

Making the demand to be present and then choosing to do it, even as it gets uncomfortable, allows the quantum entangle-ments to gift you with whatever you've been asking for. How does it get any better than that?

With every question, every choice, and every possibility, you're inviting the quantum entanglements of the entire universe to join with you to actualize what you desire.

The universe wishes to support us, but we act like we're all alone. It's as if we think the universe is an ecosystem we have to exclude ourselves from. We think we have to do everything ourselves, yet we are part of the whole. If we embrace our-selves as part of the whole without any judgment, we abso-lutely invite the whole to be part of us and we open to the uni-verse, which gives us everything we desire.

There's nothing in the entire universe fighting us, except us!

THE THIRD CALL

CLEARINGS

What have you made so vital about choosing penalties that keeps you always choosing that which will penalize you and never being the possibilities and the freedom that possibilities bring? Everything that is times a godzillion, will you destroy and uncreate it all? Right and Wrong, Good and Bad, POD and POC, All 9, Shorts, Boys, and Beyonds.

What have you made so vital about never choosing for, through, by, and with possibility that keeps you seeking right or wrong as the reason and justification for every choice you choose? Everything that is times a godzillion, will you destroy and uncreate it all? Right and Wrong, Good and Bad, POD and POC, All 9, Shorts, Boys, and Beyonds.

What future are you actualizing that you're not acknowledging? Everything that is times a godzillion, will you destroy and uncreate it all? Right and Wrong, Good and Bad, POD and POC, All 9, Shorts, Boys, and Beyonds.

All the fear you bought as true in order to limit you, will you destroy and uncreate all that? Right and Wrong, Good and Bad, POD and POC, All 9, Shorts, Boys, and Beyonds.

What fear are you using to create the limitations of what you can choose are you choosing? Everything that is times a godzillion, will you destroy and uncreate it all? Right and Wrong, Good and Bad, POD and POC, All 9, Shorts, Boys, and Beyonds.

How many choices have you chosen to avoid the knowing you could have all the time? Everything that is times a godzillion, will you destroy and uncreate it all? Right and Wrong, Good and Bad, POD and POC, All 9, Shorts, Boys, and Beyonds.

How many choices have you made not to be, so you can live in this do-do reality? Everything that is times a godzillion, will you destroy and uncreate it all? Right and Wrong, Good and Bad, POD and POC, All 9, Shorts, Boys, and Beyonds.

How many choices have you made not to perceive in order to make sure that you don't have to have total awareness? Everything that is times a godzillion, will you destroy and uncreate it all? Right and Wrong, Good and Bad, POD and POC, All 9, Shorts, Boys, and Beyonds.

How many choices have you made not to receive to make sure you get to struggle through this reality? Everything that is times a godzillion, will you destroy and uncreate it all? Right and Wrong, Good and Bad, POD and POC, All 9, Shorts, Boys, and Beyonds.

THE FOURTH CALL

Without Gratitude You Can't Receive

*You need to have gratitude for the fact
that you have many possibilities so
the quantum entanglements of the
universe can contribute to you.*

SO MANY CHOICES! WHAT DO I CHOOSE?

Gary: Hello, everyone. Does anyone have a question?

Call Participant: What do you do when you feel blank in front of choices that are available to you?

Gary: People choose blankness because they figure if they're blank, they can't make a mistake. Ask: "What energy, space, and consciousness can I be that will allow me never to choose blankness as the source of choice for all eternity?"

How many of you try to avoid mistakes by making yourself as blank as you possibly can at every choice? Everything that is times a godzillion, will you destroy and uncreate it all? Right and Wrong, Good and Bad, POD and POC, All 9, Shorts, Boys, and Beyonds.

Call Participant: It seems like there's a fine line between feeling blank and not being motivated or not having the same old motivations I used to have. Those two things feel similar to me, because I really don't have a whole lot of motivation any more.

Gary: There is no such thing as motivation. That's an invention you use to create need in your world. When you run out of need, you get choice. When you have choice, you eventually get to the point where you say, "Wow, so many choices! What do I choose?" not "Oh, I can't choose because there are too many choices."

- What invention are you using to create the motivation you are choosing? Everything that is times a godzillion, will you destroy and uncreate it all? Right and Wrong, Good and Bad, POD and POC, All 9, Shorts, Boys, and Beyonds.

WHAT IF YOU'VE ALREADY MADE A CHOICE?

Call Participant: Choice sometimes feels blank to me, too. I know things are happening, it's just … there's confusion there.

Gary: What if you've already made a choice? Would that then feel like blankness? The more aware you get, the more you look at something and say, "Oh! That!" You don't have to ask for a choice; you don't have to look *at* a choice. You already *know* where you want to go. You know what you want to create, you know what you're going to generate. You're already there. The more aware you get, the more you're going to be there before you even start.

How many of you try to avoid mistakes by making yourself as blank as you can at every choice? Everything that is times a godzillion, will you destroy and uncreate it all? Right and Wrong, Good and Bad, POD and POC, All 9, Shorts, Boys, and Beyonds.

How many of you try to avoid mistakes by making yourself as blank as you can at every choice? Everything that is times a godzillion, will you destroy and uncreate it all? Right and Wrong, Good and Bad, POD and POC, All 9, Shorts, Boys, and Beyonds.

RECEIVING ALL OF IT

Gary: You have to start acknowledging that you already know where you want to go. You have to start acknowledging that you've already chosen. People are always saying things like, "My dad never acknowledged me. My mum never acknowledged me. My family never acknowledged me." Well, guess what? You have to start acknowledging others so you can develop the standard version of acknowledgment. If you're always looking for someone else to do something for you, it's because you're not *being* it. That's why you can't receive it. What you cannot *be*, you cannot *receive*, whether it's acknowledgment, money, wealth, fame, fortune, or anything else.

Call Participant: When you said that, I realized for the first time that I'm actually very grateful for my family.

Gary: I'm glad. That's a new point of view.

Call Participant: It's totally a new point of view and it makes me smile. I am where I am and I made that choice, and it has created a lot.

Gary: It has created *you*. Instead of being somebody who's trying to be like your family, you required you to be *you* and find *you*.

Call Participant: Absolutely. There's no way I could say, "My family is wonderful. They are kind and rich, and I'm happy." I had to choose. I had to learn to choose.

Gary: Yes, you had to learn to choose. Developing the ability to receive all of it requires you to develop the ability to be grateful. One of the greatest talents you can have in life is gratitude, but it's one of the least desired talents here on planet Earth.

If you have gratitude, only then can you have receiving. The only way you're going to get it is by choosing that which creates gratitude and more gratitude in your life, until you can receive. Without gratitude, you cannot receive. So if you're having trouble with money, as an example, you have to ask:

- What gratitude do I have for money?

- What gratitude do I have for my life that would allow me to receive more money?

Acknowledge the gratitude you have and more choices become available to you.

Everything you're unwilling to perceive, know, be, and receive about what you have gratitude for, will you destroy and uncreate it all? Right and Wrong, Good and Bad, POD and POC, All 9, Shorts, Boys, and Beyonds.

Call Participant: There must be something in there for me because I went blank for half of what you said.

Gary: Who or what do you have gratitude for?

Call Participant: The first thing that came to my awareness was the Earth.

Gary: If you're grateful for the Earth, how do you express it? Do you exhibit lots of joy when you're in touch with and on the Earth?

Call Participant: Yeah, all the time.

Gary: Making the demand to be present and then choosing to do it, even as it gets uncomfortable, allows the quantum entanglements to gift you with whatever you've been asking for. How does it get any better than that? All of the things you do begin to create much more than you acknowledge.

Are you acknowledging that's gratitude for the Earth?

Call Participant: I never acknowledged that it was gratitude for the Earth. Now I will do that. Thank you.

BE GRATEFUL FOR THE GIFT YOU ARE

Gary: There's a Texas teenager named Perry Alagappan whose grandparents live in India. When he was visiting them, he saw waste from electronic technology being dumped into the water. He developed a ground-breaking $20 water purifier that takes the heavy metal contaminants from electronic waste out of the water, and he insists on making the filter available to everyone. He was recognized in 2015 at World Water Week in Stockholm for his remarkable invention. Pretty amazing, right? He has gratitude for the Earth and gratitude for his gift. He's willing to create greater. This is the place the world has to go.

Call Participant: It seems to me, that he honored his capacity to know what he knew to be true, for him, and didn't get hung up in what this reality says is possible or impossible or who he should be or who he should not be, or any of those things. That's a capacity we all have, isn't it, if we're willing to choose it?

Gary: Yes, and to choose that, you have to be willing to have an awareness of yourself and be grateful for you as the gift you actually are.

How many of you have gifts that you don't have gratitude for that doesn't allow you to expand them? Everything that is times a godzillion, will you destroy and uncreate it all? Right and Wrong, Good and Bad, POD and POC, All 9, Shorts, Boys, and Beyonds.

What capacity and brilliance do you have that you're not acknowledging that if you would acknowledge it would create a whole different universe? Everything that is times a godzillion, will you destroy and uncreate it all? Right and Wrong, Good and Bad, POD and POC, All 9, Shorts, Boys, and Beyonds.

What ability do you have that you have no gratitude for that if you had gratitude for it would allow you to change the world? Everything that is times a godzillion, will you destroy and uncreate it all? Right and Wrong, Good and Bad, POD and POC, All 9, Shorts, Boys, and Beyonds.

Call Participant: What would it take to be the gift of me?

Gary: At some point, you're going to get that you are a gift, and you can't get it until you can get it! That's the way it works. You get it when you get it; that's all there is.

When you have gratitude for the gifts you are and the gifts you have, nothing else is necessary. I have gratitude for the gift I have with horses and as a result, I get results with horses that few people do.

Call Participant: I've been grateful for my cookie-making ability and I've always made great cookies.

Gary: Yes, I've been grateful for the cookies you make as a Christmas present. They are very nice. I probably shouldn't have said that, because now I will get 270,000 cookies, and there's only so much shelf life for homemade cookies, so send me money instead of cookies, okay? I like money even better than cookies.

Call Participant: Would what you're saying apply to having gratitude for your clients? Would that create the same thing?

Gary: When you're grateful for your clients, you might find you have even more of them. I'm grateful for every session people have with me, because every session awakens some new possibility.

WHAT WOULD BE AN INTERESTING THING TO PUT HERE?

Call Participant: I'm in a space that feels like a blank canvas. You're telling us to acknowledge what our gifts are and appreciate those, so that we can actually create with those, and I'm…

Gary: If you have a blank slate, it gives you something to paint on. You don't have to just sit there and look at it. You can ask:

- What would I like to create?
- What would be an interesting thing to put here?

Call Participant: I have not discovered that yet. When you say, "Acknowledge your gifts, acknowledge what is really fun for you, acknowledge the things that you love to do," is that the place I can begin to create from once I acknowledge those things and know what they are?

Gary: Yes, but you don't have to *try* to know what they are, because you already *know* what they are. You just haven't been choosing them intentionally. You have those things available to you. When are you going to choose them?

Call Participant: I'm ready!

THE WILLINGNESS TO CHOOSE MORE

Call Participant: I have been looking for some Access classes I would like to take, and when I ask, "Should I take this class now or later?" for almost every single one, I get, "Now! Now! Now!"

Gary: Are you truly willing to wait for anything?

Call Participant: No. (laughs)

Gary: So what does that tell you about you?

Call Participant: That I'm willing to choose more and more and more.

Gary: Yes. If you were willing to acknowledge that you want to choose more and more, you'd see that you've already made a choice: You want more and more, right?

Call Participant: Right.

Gary: What if you were willing to acknowledge that you want more and then you asked: "What do I have to be to get everything I want, the way I want it, as soon as I want it?"

Call Participant: (laughs) I'm going to run that one! I'm totally running that one!

Gary: Okay, run that, because you keep trying to "do" or "not do" things.

Call Participant: Yeah. I keep trying to put things in order.

Gary: Stop trying to create order in your life. One of the greatest gifts all of you have is the ability to create from chaos, which means you can randomly choose a dozen things, put them together and somehow they will all work out. But rather than using that capacity, you keep trying to create order and sanity according to this reality's idea of sanity.

Everything that is times a godzillion, will you destroy and uncreate it all? Right and Wrong, Good and Bad, POD and POC, All 9, Shorts, Boys, and Beyonds.

What capacity and brilliance do you have that you're not acknowledging that if you would acknowledge it would create a whole dif-

ferent universe? Everything that is times a godzillion, will you de-stroy and uncreate it all? Right and Wrong, Good and Bad, POD and POC, All 9, Shorts, Boys, and Beyonds.

What ability do you have that you have no gratitude for that if you had gratitude for it would change the entire world? Everything that is times a godzillion, will you destroy and uncreate it all? Right and Wrong, Good and Bad, POD and POC, All 9, Shorts, Boys, and Be-yonds.

ARE YOU WILLING TO BE A VOICE BEYOND REALITY?

Gary: Here's another process:

What energy, space, and consciousness can you be that would allow you to be a voice beyond reality with total ease? Everything that doesn't allow that times a godzillion, will you destroy and uncreate it all? Right and Wrong, Good and Bad, POD and POC, All 9, Shorts, Boys, and Beyonds.

Call Participant: Why does that make me cry?

Gary: Well, it doesn't make *you* cry; it probably makes *your body* cry. Are you willing to be a voice beyond this reality?

Call Participant: What does it mean to be a voice beyond this reality?

Gary: It means that when you speak, you'll speak to what people can hear, or what people desire, or what you want them to hear, or what the world might hear when it's ready, if you can speak from when it's ready.

Call Participant: For me it's that one.

Gary: When the world's ready, you'll be able to speak.

Call Participant: Oh my goodness. I have to wait for the world to be ready before I can speak?

Gary: Yes, but did you notice the change in your voice right then?

Call Participant: I did! It's different. Totally!

Gary: Apparently, the world can hear what you have to say. Keep it a secret, though! Not that this would apply to any of the rest of you...

Call Participants: (laughter)

Gary: What energy, space, and consciousness can you be that would allow you to be a voice beyond reality with total ease? Everything that doesn't allow that times a godzillion, will you destroy and uncreate it all? Right and Wrong, Good and Bad, POD and POC, All 9, Shorts, Boys, and Beyonds.

> *What are you grateful for that you've never acknowledged that if you allowed yourself to acknowledge it would allow you to receive what you've never received? Everything that is times a godzillion, will you destroy and uncreate it all? Right and Wrong, Good and Bad, POD and POC, All 9, Shorts, Boys, and Beyonds.*

And remember, to totally *receive*, you have to be willing to totally *be*.

> *What are you refusing to be that if you would not refuse to be it would actually allow you to receive everything in totality? Every-*

thing that is times a godzillion, will you destroy and uncreate it all?
Right and Wrong, Good and Bad, POD and POC, All 9, Shorts, Boys,
and Beyonds.

BEING A CATALYST FOR CHANGE

Call Participant: Would you talk about choice and being a catalyst for change?

Gary: Being a catalyst for change is the willingness to see what you see and do what you do and have no point of view whether anybody goes along with you. In fact, if you have no point of view about whether anybody goes along with you, everybody will want to go along and go with you.

If you are trying to get people to go along, you're looking for something or someone to validate you in some way. That is not going to create your life.

I do what I do whether anyone else validates it or not. The weird part about it is, in doing all these things, I get validations from all kinds of people and I don't care. When I cared, I never got validations; I got criticism all the time. When I wanted validation, I got criticism. When I no longer cared about criticism, I got validation.

Call Participant: What you just said is awesome. I wish I knew what question to ask right now.

Gary: The question you want to ask is: "Where am I looking for validation and where am I unwilling to receive judgment?"

When you're unwilling to receive judgment, you look for somebody to validate you to prove that the judgment isn't real. And why do you do that? Because you've made the judgments more real than you.

Call Participant: (laughs) Who me?! It really just comes down to awareness and choice in that case, doesn't it?

Gary: Ultimately it comes down to choice and possibility, because more than anything else, you want to be aware of what your possibilities are, and choice always gives you an awareness of what's possible.

EXPANDING YOUR CAPACITY FOR CHOICE

Call Participant: I feel like I don't know what to choose anymore.

Gary: Are you aware that you have spent your life trying to look at both sides of every argument?

Call Participant: Well, yeah. How am I going to win if I don't look at both sides?

Gary: Oops! Is it about winning and losing? That's judgment. You've got to be willing to allow yourself to have your awareness. By looking at a choice, you know what it is going to create and you can choose whether to do it or not. You have to learn to have gratitude for the ability to choose and to have gratitude for what you can choose. That's when new possibilities show up, along with an awareness of what you choose and how it works.

Every time you choose something, you expand your capacity for choice. Through choice you learn how to expand the elements of life you wish to have.

Call Participant: So in those moments where I go to logic, I feel like I have no choice?

Gary: You've chosen to have no choice so you don't have to make a decision that can be wrong. That's being in judgment. You've chosen judgment of you rather than possibility for you.

Call Participant: Wow. Thank you.

YOUR CHOICE IS GOING TO CREATE A DIFFERENCE

Gary: What if you started to choose your life and your reality from:

- Okay, I have a choice.
- What is this choice going to create?

What if you started looking for everything that got created by every choice? Would anything be different? Or would everything be different?

Call Participant: Everything would be different.

Gary: That's what you've got to realize. Your choice is going to create a difference. Ask: "What is the difference I am going to create with the choice I am choosing?"

CREATING A DIFFERENT REALITY ON THIS PLANET

You are the creators of the future that has not yet actualized on planet Earth but that will exist because of every choice you've made. What you're choosing today is going to create, in 500 years, a totally different reality on this planet. It's going to become a place of possibility. It's going to become a place in which people are not trying to use, abuse, and cut everything up.

Dain and I were talking the other day about how when people who have money die, their family members, in order to get their share, divide everything up and sell it off. They don't try to create. They're not interested in creation because they've never created their lives. Their idea of creation is waiting until someone dies, so they can have.

But you, by your choices, are already creating another universe in which a universe beyond this reality is beginning to actualize. You may think that something is the future and such-and-such a thing is going to happen. What if you were willing to look from a different point of view? What if, by putting pictures out there in the world that a certain thing is going to happen, you're making it happen?

That's the way the universe really is. If you put into the universe that something is going to be a disaster, that's what gets created. If you put in the universe, "Hey, there's a different possibility," that's what gets created.

By the choices you make daily, you are creating a reality that has never been here before. By every choice you make to choose more consciousness, to be more aware of even the slightest thing in the world, you are creating a different reality from the destruction and disaster that have been predicted—the wars, the pestilence, and the famines.

I find it interesting that people have stopped talking about Armageddon the way they used to. Have you noticed that? Armageddon used to be a dynamic conversation. Every right wing

Christian was talking about Armageddon and what would happen if we didn't prepare for it.

They've now dropped that conversation and they're going to "God loves us. He won't let this happen." You are creating by the choices you make. You're creating a reality that is beginning to actualize on planet Earth, but it's only beginning. The more you choose for possibility, the more dynamic it will be. *You* are the source of the future that has not yet come to fruition.

> *Everywhere you have not chosen to be the source of creating a reality that has not yet come to fruition and everywhere you think you can't be that powerful when you are, will you destroy and uncreate all that? Right and Wrong, Good and Bad, POD and POC, All 9, Shorts, Boys, and Beyonds.*

We're changing the universe by what we're doing. Earth may end up being the golden planet of peace, which is not a mineable commodity. It's already in the works and you guys are the ones who are creating it.

It's happening not because of light beings, ETs, Pleiadians, places outside the universe, or any of the stuff you hear people talk about, because those things assume there's somebody outside of us who's going to save our asses. Each one of us, by every choice we make for a greater possibility, is saving our asses and creating a reality in which our asses are not going to be the issue.

You have a choice to acknowledge this building block for a greater possibility and a greater world. It's the gift that each and every one of you are, every frigging day.

I'm very grateful for all of you. Thank you, everyone.

Please remember these things:

- You need to choose in order to become aware.
- You need to ask a question in order to know what to choose.
- You need to choose in order to see what's possible.
- You need to have gratitude for the fact that you have that many possibilities so the quantum entanglements of the universe can contribute to you.

THE FOURTH CALL

CLEARINGS

How many of you try to avoid mistakes by making yourself as blank as you possibly can at every possible choice? Everything that is times a godzillion, will you destroy and uncreate it all? Right and Wrong, Good and Bad, POD and POC, All 9, Shorts, Boys, and Beyonds.

What invention are you using to create the motivation you are choosing? Everything that is times a godzillion, will you destroy and uncreate it all? Right and Wrong, Good and Bad, POD and POC, All 9, Shorts, Boys, and Beyonds.

Everything you're unwilling to perceive, know, be, and receive about what you have gratitude for, will you destroy and uncreate it all? Right and Wrong, Good and Bad, POD and POC, All 9, Shorts, Boys, and Beyonds.

How many of you have gifts that you don't have gratitude for that doesn't allow you to expand them? Everything that is times a godzillion, will you destroy and uncreate it all? Right and Wrong, Good and Bad, POD and POC, All 9, Shorts, Boys, and Beyonds.

What capacity and brilliance do you have that you're not acknowledging that if you would acknowledge it would create a whole different universe? Everything that is times a godzillion, will you destroy and uncreate it all? Right and Wrong, Good and Bad, POD and POC, All 9, Shorts, Boys, and Beyonds.

What ability do you have that you have no gratitude for that if you had gratitude for it would allow you to change the world? Everything that is times a godzillion, will you destroy and uncreate it all? Right and Wrong, Good and Bad, POD and POC, All 9, Shorts, Boys, and Beyonds.

What energy, space, and consciousness can you be that would allow you to be a voice beyond reality with total ease? Everything that doesn't allow that times a godzillion, will you destroy and uncreate it all? Right and Wrong, Good and Bad, POD and POC, All 9, Shorts, Boys, and Beyonds.

What are you grateful for that you've never acknowledged that if you allowed yourself to acknowledge it would allow you to receive what you've never received? Everything that is times a godzillion, will you destroy and uncreate it all? Right and Wrong, Good and Bad, POD and POC, All 9, Shorts, Boys, and Beyonds.

What are you refusing to be that if you would not refuse to be it would actually allow you to receive everything in totality? Everything that is times a godzillion, will you destroy and uncreate it all? Right and Wrong, Good and Bad, POD and POC, All 9, Shorts, Boys, and Beyonds.

Everywhere you have not chosen to be the source of creating a reality that has not yet come to fruition and everywhere you think you can't be that powerful when you are, will you destroy and uncreate all that? Right and Wrong, Good and Bad, POD and POC, All 9, Shorts, Boys, and Beyonds.

The Access Consciousness Clearing Statement®

You are the only one who can unlock the points of view that have you trapped.

What I am offering here with the clearing process is a tool you can use to change the energy of the points of view that have you locked into unchanging situations.

Throughout this book, I ask a lot of questions, and some of those questions might twist your head around a little bit. That's my intention. The questions I ask are designed to get your mind out of the picture so you can get to the *energy* of a situation.

Once the question has twisted your head around and brought up the energy of a situation, I ask if you are willing to destroy and uncreate that energy—because stuck energy is the source of barriers and limitations. Destroying and uncreating that energy will open the door to new possibilities for you.

This is your opportunity to say, "Yes, I'm willing to let go of whatever is holding that limitation in place."

That will be followed by some weird-speak we call the clearing statement:

Right and Wrong, Good and Bad, POD and POC, All 9, Shorts, Boys, and Beyonds.

With the clearing statement, we're going back to the energy of the limitations and barriers that have been created. We're looking at the energies that keep us from moving forward and expanding into all of the spaces that we would like to go. The clearing statement addresses the energies that are creating the limitations and contractions in our life.

The more you run the clearing statement, the deeper it goes and the more layers and levels it can unlock for you. If a lot of energy comes up for you in response to a question, you may wish to repeat the process numerous times until the subject being addressed is no longer an issue for you.

You don't have to understand the words of the clearing statement for it to work because it's about the energy. However, if you're interested in knowing what the words mean, some brief definitions are given below.

Right and Wrong, Good and Bad is shorthand for: What's right, good, perfect, and correct about this? What's wrong, mean, vicious, terrible, bad, and awful about this? The short version of these questions is: Right and wrong, good and bad. It is the things that we consider right, good, perfect, and/or correct that stick us the most. We do not wish to let go of them since we decided that we have them right.

POD stands for the **P**oint **of D**estruction; all the ways you have been destroying yourself in order to keep whatever you're clearing in existence.

POC stands for the **P**oint **of C**reation of the thoughts, feelings, and emotions immediately preceding your decision to lock the energy in place.

Sometimes people say, "POD and POC it," which is simply shorthand for the longer statement. When you "POD and POC" something, it is like pulling the bottom card out of a house of cards. The whole thing falls down.

All 9 stands for the nine different ways you have created this item as a limitation in your life. They are the layers of thoughts, feelings, emotions, and points of view that create the limitation as solid and real.

Shorts is the short version of a much longer series of questions that include: What's meaningful about this? What's meaning-less about this? What's the punishment for this? What's the reward for this?

Boys stands for energetic structures called nucleated spheres. Basically these have to do with those areas of our life where we've tried to handle something continuously with no effect. There are at least thirteen different kinds of these spheres, which are collectively called "the boys." A nucleated sphere looks like the bubbles you create when you blow in one of those kids' bubble pipes that has multiple chambers. It creates a huge mass of bubbles, and when you pop one bubble, the other bubbles fill in the space.

Have you ever tried to peel away the layers of an onion when you were trying to get to the core of an issue, but you could never get there? That's because it wasn't an onion; it was a nucleated sphere.

Beyonds are feelings or sensations that stop your heart, stop your breath, or stop your willingness to look at possibilities. Beyonds are what occur when you are in shock. We have lots of areas in our life where we freeze up. Anytime you freeze up, it's a beyond holding you captive. That's the difficulty with a beyond: it stops you from being present. The beyonds include everything that is beyond belief, reality, imagination, conception, perception, rationalization, forgiveness, as well as all the other beyonds. They are usually feelings and sensations, rarely emotions, and never thoughts.

CPSIA information can be obtained
at www.ICGtesting.com
Printed in the USA
BVHW031258140619
551051BV00001B/64/P

9 781634 931557